PRESIDENTS' DAY

 Mary Dodson Wade

Enslow Publishing
101 W. 23rd Street
Suite 240
New York, NY 10011
USA

enslow.com

Published in 2017 by Enslow Publishing, LLC.
101 W. 23rd Street, Suite 240, New York, NY 10011

Library of Congress Cataloging-in-Publication Data

Names: Wade, Mary Dodson, author.
Title: Presidents' Day / Mary Dodson Wade.
Description: New York, NY : Enslow Publishing, 2017. | Series: The story of our holidays | Includes bibliographical references and index. | Audience: Age 8 and up. | Audience: Grade 4 to 6.
Identifiers: LCCN 2016022183| ISBN 9780766083486 (library bound) | ISBN 9780766083455 (pbk.) | ISBN 9780766083479 (6-pack)
Subjects: LCSH: Presidents' Day—Juvenile literature. | Washington, George, 1732–1799—Juvenile literature. | Lincoln, Abraham, 1809–1865—Juvenile literature. | Presidents—United States—History—Juvenile literature.
Classification: LCC E176.8 .W329 2016 | DDC 394.261—dc23
LC record available at https://lccn.loc.gov/2016022183

Printed in China

To Our Readers: We have done our best to make sure all websites in this book were active and appropriate when we went to press. However, the author and the publisher have no control over and assume no liability for the material available on those websites or on any websites they may link to. Any comments or suggestions can be sent by e-mail to customerservice@enslow.com.

Portions of this book originally appeared in the book *Presidents' Day: Honoring the Birthdays of Washington and Lincoln*.

Contents

Every four years, the United States holds a presidential election. Every adult in the country has a voice in who the next leader will be.

Chapter 1

Celebrate the President

Presidents' Day is a great way to honor the leader of our country. We celebrate this special holiday on the third Monday of February each year. Two of our most famous presidents were born in February—George Washington and Abraham Lincoln.

The United States is a democracy. In a democracy, people choose the country's leader. We elect our president by voting for a candidate. There can be two or more candidates who want the job of being president. The one with the most votes wins.

The winter spent at Valley Forge was a hard one for Washington and his troops.

We have been celebrating United States presidents for more than two hundred years. It started as a way to honor our first president, George Washington.

Washington's Birthday

Before Washington became president, he led the American army. Americans were fighting to be free from Great Britain. Washington's soldiers spent the terrible winter of 1778 at Valley Forge, Pennsylvania. They were cold, hungry, and unhappy. The army band cheered up everyone by playing music to celebrate Washington's birthday.

Even after Washington was no longer president, people celebrated his birthday with dances and parties. In 1885, President Chester A. Arthur signed a bill that gave government workers a holiday on Washington's birthday.

By that time, some states were also celebrating Abraham Lincoln's birthday. That made two holidays in February.

Making It a Holiday

In 1968, Congress set the celebration of Washington's Birthday on the third Monday in February. The Monday holiday gave government

Here Barack Obama, the forty-fourth president, is sworn in for his second term of office. Presidents' Day honors all the presidents who have served the United States.

workers a three-day weekend. Three years later, President Richard Nixon made the holiday include all our presidents. He signed a proclamation setting Presidents' Day on the third Monday in February. On Presidents' Day we honor all our presidents, not just Washington and Lincoln.

Chapter 2

Honoring Our First President

George Washington did not plan to be a president. When he was born on February 22, 1732, he was a British citizen. There was no United States of America.

Road to the Presidency

Washington lived in the Virginia Colony. His father owned huge farms called plantations. One of these plantations was Mount Vernon. Washington's older brother became owner after their father died.

George Washington grew tall and strong. At age seventeen, he became a surveyor. He measured land and made maps in places that had no roads or towns. Later, French soldiers tried

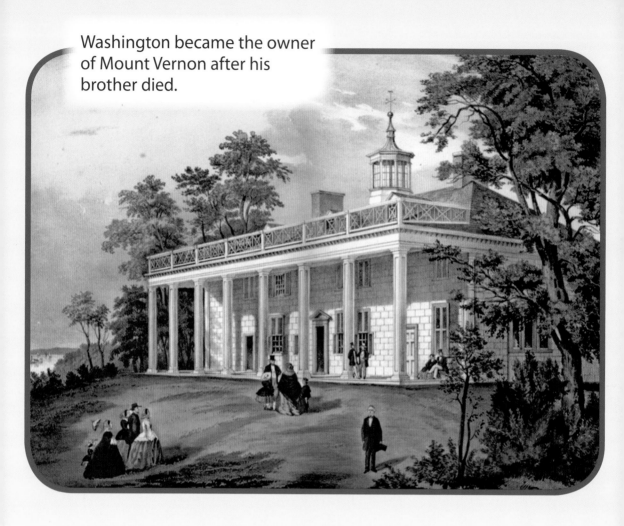

Washington became the owner of Mount Vernon after his brother died.

to take land where British settlers lived. Washington joined the British army to fight the French.

After his brother died, Washington became owner of Mount Vernon. He loved this place. He planted different kinds of crops and did things to make it better.

Washington married Martha Dandridge Custis. Her first husband had died. She had a son, John (Jacky) Custis. Her daughter was named Martha, but they called her Patsy. Washington bought Jacky clothes and books from England. He bought a piano for Patsy.

Later Martha's two grandchildren lived with them. But the Washingtons never had any children of their own.

Washington's manners impressed people. Instead of shaking hands with

Martha Dandridge Custis married George Washington on January 6, 1759.

his guests, he bowed to them. But he rarely smiled. His teeth were bad. Doctors carved him new ones from cow and hippopotamus teeth. The false teeth opened by a metal spring.

Washington helped make Virginia's laws. Then, the British government put a tax on things the colonists bought. Washington joined the protest against the taxes. Finally, the colonies went to war

This image captures a famous victory over the British, when Washington crossed the Delaware River and led a surprise attack against some soldiers fighting for the British.

This is one of several portraits of George Washington painted by Gilbert Stuart.

against Great Britain. Washington led the American soldiers. The Americans kept fighting until they finally won.

Americans did not want a king as ruler. Instead, people could vote to choose their country's leader.

A New Nation, a New Leader

Everyone voted for George Washington to be president of the United States of America. Then people chose him again. Many wanted him to be president a third time. Washington refused. He felt it was not right for one person to run the country for a long time.

Several artists painted George Washington. One of the best-known portraits was done by American painter Gilbert Stuart. Washington posed for the portrait a year before he left the presidency. That likeness is on our one-dollar bill.

After being president, Washington was glad to return home. But three years later he died, on December 14, 1799. He and Martha Washington are buried at Mount Vernon.

Washington gave our country a strong beginning. He is called the "father of our country."

Chapter 3

Washington's Big Plans

George Washington had great plans for our country. He wanted to build a capital. This city would be a special place for the government. Maryland and Virginia gave land for the new capital. This area is called the District of Columbia. It is not part of any state. Washington, DC, is named in honor of our first president.

Washington asked Pierre L'Enfant to plan the new capital. L'Enfant laid out a beautiful city. It had long, extra-wide streets and space for large government buildings and parks. He chose one hill for the capitol building. He put the president's home on another. The president's home is now called the White House because of its color.

This is Pierre Charles L'Enfant's plan for the city of Washington. You can see the Potomac River at the bottom and the grid showing where he wanted all the roads to go.

Some people wanted to change L'Enfant's plans for the city. He became angry. He took his plans and left. Andrew Ellicott and his helper Benjamin Banneker had surveyed land for the District of Columbia. They remembered L'Enfant's plans and completed the project.

George Washington never lived in the city that has his name. It took ten years to build. He was no longer president.

George Washington made a choice about what the president should be called. Many countries had kings. Some people wanted to

This is the White House as it looks today.

call him "His Highness the President of the United States of America and Protector of their Liberties." George Washington did not like that idea. He just wanted to be called "Mr. President."

Another important thing happened while Washington was president. Amendments were added to the Constitution. The Constitution is the set of laws that governs our country. The first ten amendments are called the Bill of Rights. These amendments gave Americans certain personal freedoms.

The Post Office was also created to make sure letters were delivered. Before that, people had to find someone to carry letters for them.

All these things made our country better.

Chapter 4

The President Who Saved Our Country

Nobody would have guessed that Abraham Lincoln would become president. He was born in a log cabin in Kentucky on February 12, 1809. Lincoln's father was honest and worked hard, but they were very poor.

The family moved to Indiana when Abraham Lincoln was about seven. He helped his father clear forests. He became strong splitting logs.

His mother, Nancy Hanks Lincoln, taught him to read. She died when he was nine. Lincoln's stepmother, Sarah

Abraham Lincoln grew up on the frontier in Kentucky and Indiana.

Johnson Lincoln, also encouraged him to learn. He did not go to school very long. But he learned lots by reading books.

When Lincoln was twenty-one years old, the family moved to Illinois. He studied a friend's law books. He become a lawyer and worked hard to help the people who came to him. Lincoln married Mary Todd. They had four sons—Robert, Edward (Eddie), William (Willie), and Thomas (Tad).

People in Illinois elected him as their congressman. After that, he was a senator. He made strong speeches against slavery. He felt slavery was wrong. It divided the nation. He said, "A house divided against itself cannot stand."

Lincoln is shown being sworn in for his second term as president in this drawing.

In 1860, the new Republican Party chose Abraham Lincoln as its candidate for president. Some people in the South did not like his stand against slavery. Several states left the Union when he was elected. They formed the Confederate States of America. For five long years Americans fought each other in the bitter Civil War.

A terrible battle took place at Gettysburg, Pennsylvania, in 1863. Many soldiers from both sides died. President Lincoln went there to dedicate the cemetery. The main speaker talked for two hours. Then Lincoln made a very short speech.

He honored the soldiers who had died for their country. He urged people to keep the nation together. He wanted to make sure that the "government of the people by the people for the people shall not perish from the earth."

People clapped politely. Lincoln thought nobody cared about what he said. Today Lincoln's Gettysburg speech is called one of the greatest ever made.

That same year, President Lincoln made two important proclamations. The Emancipation Proclamation freed slaves. The other proclamation made Thanksgiving Day an official holiday. We take time each November to be thankful for the good things we have.

People elected Lincoln a second time. But he did not serve long. The Confederacy surrendered, and the Civil War ended.

A week later, President and Mrs. Lincoln went to Ford's Theater in Washington. They were watching a play when John Wilkes Booth

Address delivered at the dedication of the cemetery at Gettysburg.

Four score and seven years ago our fathers brought forth on this continent, a new nation, conceived in Liberty, and dedicated to the proposition that all men are created equal.

Now we are engaged in a great civil war, testing whether that nation, or any nation so conceived and so dedicated, can long endure. We are met on a great battlefield of that war. We have come to dedicate a portion of that field, as a final resting place for those who here gave their lives that that nation might live. It is altogether fitting and proper that we should do this.

But, in a larger sense, we can not dedicate — we can not consecrate — we can not hallow — this ground. The brave men, living and dead, who struggled here have consecrated it, far above our poor power to add or detract. The world will little note, nor long remember what we say here, but it can never forget what they did here. It is for us the living, rather, to be dedicated here to the unfinished work which they who fought here have thus far so nobly advanced. It is rather for us to be here dedicated to the great task remaining before us — that from these honored dead we take increased devotion to that cause for which they gave the last full measure of devotion — that we here highly resolve that these dead shall not have died in vain — that this nation, under God, shall have a new birth of freedom — and that government of the people, by the people, for the people, shall not perish from the earth.

Abraham Lincoln.

November 19. 1863.

This is the Gettysburg Address, the speech Lincoln gave to honor soldiers at Gettysburg.

shot the president. Lincoln died the next day. A train carried his body on a long trip back to Illinois. He is buried in Springfield.

Abraham Lincoln was the first president to be photographed at his inauguration. But we remember him for his honesty and his efforts to hold our nation together.

Chapter 5

A Parade of Presidents

By 2017 America has elected forty-five American presidents. They are as different as the citizens of our country.

Some like Washington were wealthy. Some were lawyers. Some of them had been state governors or members of Congress before being elected. John Quincy Adams became a congressman *after* being president.

Some presidents had been soldiers, and several were generals. Others were teachers. Ronald Reagan had been a movie actor. Andrew Johnson had been a tailor, and Harry Truman sold clothing.

Ronald Reagan (1911–2004) appeared in 53 Hollywood films from the 1930s to the 1960s. He was the governor of California before serving as the 40th president from 1981 to 1989.

Americans honor their presidents on Presidents' Day. But we especially remember George Washington and Abraham Lincoln because of what they did to help our country.

Cooking on Presidents' Day

Many people associate George Washington with cherry trees, and Washington, DC—home of the president—is famous for its many beautiful cherry trees, too. So what better dessert to make in honor of Presidents' Day than cherry pie?

Cherry Pie Ingredients:

2 (12 oz) cans pitted cherries
1 tbs cornstarch
¾ cups of sugar
premade pie crust

Directions:

1. Preheat oven to 350°F. Grease a 9x11" baking dish.
2. Carefully unfold your pie crust. There will be two in a package. You can use a rolling pin to flatten it out, if desired. Place one crust in the bottom of your pie dish, pressing the edges and bottom of the dish to avoid air bubbles. Poke the bottom of the crust with a fork.
3. In a large bowl, combine cherries, cornstarch, and sugar. Be sure and keep all the juice from the cans of cherries.
4. Pour the cherry mixture into the pie dish.
5. Take the second pie crust and flatten it out with a rolling pin covered in flour. Cut the crust into 1-inch strips.
6. Place strips, about one inch apart, on top of the cherry mixture (you should be able to make about five lines across the pie). Turn the pie dish so that the lines are now going up and down. Place another set of lines of dough, still about one inch apart, across. These lines create what is called a lattice crust.
7. Cut off any excess dough that might be hanging off the side of the pie dish.
8. Bake for 15–20 minutes, or until cherries are bubbling in their juice and the crust has turned golden brown.

27

* Adult supervision required.

Presidents' Day Craft

The president of the United States tries to make the country better. Make this booklet to show what you would do if you were president.

3 strips of plain white paper, 8½ inches by 4½ inches
pen or pencil
ruler
scissors
stapler
red and blue crayons or colored pencils, or patriotic stickers

Directions:

1. Stack the 3 strips of paper so that the edges are even.

2. Fold the paper in half, long ends together. (You now have six "pages" 4½ by 4¼ inches.)

3. Use the ruler to measure down 1½ inches from the crease. Draw a thin, straight line across the first page. Cut off the top page at this line.

4. Measure down 2 inches from the crease and draw a line on the second page. Cut off the second page at the line.

5. Measure down 2½ inches from the crease, draw a line, and cut the third page.

6. Open the pages to the middle and staple on the crease to keep pages from slipping.

7. Close the pages again. Measure down 3 inches on the fourth page, draw a line, and cut the fourth page.

8. Measure down 3½ inches on the fifth page, draw a line, and cut the fifth page. Do not cut the last page.

"If I Were President . . ." Book

9. Close the booklet. On the top page, write in big letters: "IF I WERE PRESIDENT . . ."

10. On page two, write: "I would . . ."

11. On each blank page, finish the sentence telling what you would do. Example: Ask everyone to pick up litter.

12. Decorate your book with the colors red, white, and blue and patriotic stickers, or draw your own patriotic symbols.

13. Put your picture on the last page and sign your name.

*Safety Note: Be sure to ask for help from an adult, if needed, to complete this project.

Glossary

amendments Changes that are added to something already written.

candidate A person who wants to be elected by voters.

capital A city where the government is located.

capitol A building where the government meets.

democracy A government that allows people to elect leaders by voting.

government The group of people or organizations that make and carry out laws.

portrait A picture of a person painted by an artist.

proclamation An official announcement made by a leader.

protector Someone who keeps others from harm.

surveyor A person who measures land.

Learn More

Books

Gilpin, Caroline Crosson. *George Washington*. Washington, DC: National Geographic Kids, 2014.

Hanson, Grace. *Abraham Lincoln*. Edina, MN: Abdo Kids, 2014.

Jennings, Ken, *U.S. Presidents.* New York, NY: Little Simon, 2014.

Singer, Marilyn. *Rutherford B., Who Was He?* New York, NY: Disney-Hyperion, 2015.

Websites

Presidents' Day Dilemma—Time for Kids
www.timeforkids.com/news/presidents-day-dilemma/29951
A history of the holiday and a discussion of which presidents should be included in the holiday.

Presidents' Day
www.scholastic.com/browse/article.jsp?id=11551
An overview of the Presidents' Day holiday.

Presidents' Day Facts
www.softschools.com/facts/holidays/presidents_day_facts/157/
Lots of fun facts about Presidents' Day.

Index